Oscar & Crystal Jones

Hot Dates for Married Lovers

Oscar & Crystal Jones

Hot Dates for Married Lovers

Copyright © 2014 Oscar and Crystal Jones
Published by Destiny House Publishing, LLC

International Standard Book Number:
978-1-936867-10-3

Unless otherwise stated, all scripture quotations are from The Holy Bible, New International Version. Scripture references that do not have the Bible version noted are the author's paraphrase.

Interior artwork: Morgue Files
Cover artwork: Can Stock

Editing and Cover design:

Destiny House Publishing, LLC.

ALL RIGHTS RESERVED

All rights reserved under International Copyright law. No part of this book may be reproduced or transmitted in any form or by any means: electronic, mechanical, including photocopying and recording, or by any information storage and retrieval system, without written permission from the publisher.

Printed in the United States of America

Hot Dates for Married Lovers

For information:

Destiny House Publishing, LLC
www.destinyhousepublishing.com
P.O. Box 19774 - Detroit, MI 48219

888.890.4555

DEDICATION

We would like to dedicate this book to
Our team members of Marriage For A Lifetime Ministries,
couples of Greater Works Family Ministries,
and The Love Culture Christian Center
And all of the pastoral teams of Agape International
Assoication of Churches and Parachurches.

CONTENTS

	Acknowledgments	i
1	Getting Started	Pg 3
2	First Dates	Pg 13
3	Free Dates	Pg 21
4	Dates On A Dime	Pg 31
5	Other Fun Dates	Pg 39
6	Romantic Getaways	Pg 47

ACKNOWLEDGMENTS

We would like to first and foremost acknowledge the One who makes all our ministry and books possible, Our Lord and Savior, Jesus Christ. We love you and appreciate all that you give us to give others. We recognize and are sure we could do none of this without you.
And finally, we would like to acknowledge our kids, Pastors Jake & Keila Allen who said we needed to write this book. We love you guys.

GETTING STARTED

Oscar & Crystal Jones

> Proverbs 5:18-19 NIV
>
> May your fountain be blessed, and may you rejoice in the wife of your youth.
>
> ¹⁹ A loving doe, a graceful deer— may her breasts satisfy you always,
>
> may you ever be intoxicated with her love.

Dating is foundation to a successful marriage.

Couples have to be careful of getting so busy that they don't take time to pour back into their relationship. If the marriage foundation crumbles , everything else will come down with it.

So it is imperative that couples nurture their relationship - and one of the great ways to do that is by dating your mate.

As singles, we all found dating easy. It was a natural way to connect. We would take the time to get away alone, to talk, laugh, and have fun together. We took time to discover one another, learning about our love's past and dreaming together about the future.

Discovery is an important part of the single process. However It is even more important for couples to continue dating **after** marriage. Dating allows you to connect with one another and create happy memories in your relationship. It will rekindle the romance you once had or for some just turn the fire up on an already "hot" relationship. It keeps the marriage fresh and exciting. It is also a way to give priority to the relationship.

Your spouse needs to be at the top of your priority list – After the Lord, your spouse should be next. Many couples "say' their spouse is first but it is not reflected in their schedules. The things that are important to us are the things for which we make time. Giving your spouse priority in your calendar is a way to honor him/her and a way to honor God. Priority time for your spouse means weekly date nights and occasional getaway weekends. Don't just try to fit your spouse in whenever you have "free" time. Give him/her time first before scheduling all the other "to do" items on your list. Healthy marriages give first place to their spouses.

We recommend that married couples date at least once a week. Choose one day out of seven to give attention to your relationship. Be consistent. You are building your marriage. So don't skip around...a date night this week and then not another one for three more months. That's a no-no. Establish a pattern. You will both begin to look forward to that time carved out just for the two of you. And others will respect and plan around your pre-scheduled date time.

Of course, date night does not have to

occur at night. Couples should work together to chose the time that is the best fit for them. That could be a morning rendezvous or a late afternoon get together.

For couples with children, plan ahead for a babysitter. Do not use your children as an excuse to not connect with one another. If you get 4 family members on board to babysit once a month, that will solve your problem without overtaxing one person.

Another great idea is to trade babysitting with another couple. You keep their kids the 1st and 3rd Saturday. They keep your kids the 2nd and 4th Friday. On those occasional 5th weekends, have date night at home. Put the little ones to bed early. If your children are older, give them a date night with each other. Pizza and a movie and a staunch warning not to disturb mom and dad or they forfeit their date night and must go to bed. So couples with children do not have to deprive themselves of their date night. They just have to be a little more creative.

Date nights should be fun. It is not a time to discuss heavy subjects or problems in the relationship. Save that for your husband-wife meetings. It is also not a time to discuss the children. This is usually a fall back discussion for parents who have gotten out of practice. Date night is a time to laugh and dream and reconnect.

Your family reunion, business trip, ministry trip, or outing with other couples does not qualify as date night. While those can be fun opportunities, you still need to understand that dating your spouse is intentional time alone with your spouse.

Some couples get stuck in a rut. Their date night consists of 1 or 2 activities, usually dinner and a movie. That movie is usually a RedBox event or something on television. When a couple is stuck, their idea of doing something different is actually seeing a showing at a movie theatre. Which in essence, is not different. You still have the same thing happening. The couple sits together looking at a screen. And that's not always a bad idea, but the purpose of dating is to reconnect. So look for activities that are different. Don't just do the same thing week after week. Mix it up.

Other couples may find it difficult to date one another. They may not have dated in a while or not understood the importance of date night and may have allowed their jobs, parenting, extracurricular activities, ministry and other commitments to crowd out their schedules. So if you are one of those that may find dating awkward and clumsy, the first dates section is for you. These are dating ideas that will help you ease into dating so that it becomes more comfortable for you both.

Couples may start by alternating the planning of date nights. Maybe husband can plan one week and wife can plan the following week. If one spouse is content on planning all the date nights, that's fine; just as long as you have them.

Some couples put a bunch of date night ideas in a jar and then randomly pull one out on their date night.

Another idea that some couples use is to bring in a personal date planner. It is free to arrange a personal date planner. You choose a friend or couple and ask them to plan the perfect date for you based on what they know about you. Give them a budget. In return, you will do the same for them. After the evening is planned, they will tell you the dress attire and give you a stack of envelopes with instructions in them. Each should be labeled with the time it should be opened. It gets you out of the routine and heightens your expectations. It's a fun way to enjoy one another.

So to all married couples out there. Marriage was never intended to be staling boring or miserable. God intended that we would fully enjoy one another. So, get up off the couch. Turn off the television and let the good times begin!

Oscar & Crystal Jones

FIRST DATES

For those who may find that dating is a little bit of a challenge, understand if you've been in this uncomfortable place for a while, you won't just leap out. It's going to take effort, patience, and commitment to see and feel a change. But kudos to you for wanting to get started.

Be prayerful asking God's wisdom as you move to give him glory in your marriage.

If you're not sure where to start, here are some basic dating tips to get you started:

<u>Watch your wedding video or look at old wedding photos</u>. Reminisce about your early years. Talk about your first date and your proposal. Relive the dream. Talk about how you felt on your wedding day.

<u>Watch a movie</u> that peaks both of your interest, and discuss it afterwards. Talk about your likes and dislikes. It's okay to disagree. The point is for each of you to share your views and get a peek into the other's mindset.

Create a dream board or dream book. To put together a DREAM BOOK or DREAM BOARD, you can use a 3-ring binder and paste pictures on unruled paper or colored construction paper, 3-hole punch it or put in a page protector & put in your binder. Or if you are using the board version, purchase a 3- section poster foam board.

Husband and wife should dream together and find pictures in a magazine that best show what you want for your family. Some people dream of owning a home or being debt free or travelling to some romantic destination. Others may put pictures of a dream vehicle or a dream career. Both of you should participate. Do not discourage the other from putting something in your dream book.

Over a cup of of something (hot chocolate or lemonade) talk about your dream house. Compare your dream house to where you live now. What things would you want in your new house? What would the man cave look like?

Complete a service project together.
Maybe you have a heart for children of inmates. Maybe you could put together Angel Tree boxes together. It may not sound romantic but it will get you two connecting again. Find a common project to work on.

Write a list of your favorite things.
Give a certain number. So that you both have the same number of items. Share your list with each other. Discuss it.

What person or couple in our lives who has been the most supportive of our marriage? Why did you chose this person(s)? Once you have agreed on who that person or couple is write them a thank you card, include a small gift of some sort. It could be something that the two of you make or search for together.

Conversation Starters

Spend some time in discussion getting to know each other. Couples who communicate more, connect more. Dig deep for the treasures of your spouse's heart.

<u>What one place have you always wanted to visit and why?</u> If possible, make a plan to visit that place within the next 2 years. Check out airline rates and hotel

accommodations.

<u>What has been the best day of your life thus far?</u> What were you doing? And why was this your best day? Don't get upset if your spouse doesn't give the answer you were hoping. That is not the purpose of this exercise. The purpose is to discover new things about one another.

<u>As your spouse, what is one thing I can do to make your life better</u>? This is not an opportunity to criticize but an opportunity to bless each other. Look at it as such.

~~~~

<u>What can I do to better support you in our marriage this month?</u>

<u>One of the most memorable things you have ever done for me is…</u>

<u>Without you, I never would have….</u>

<u>What would be your "dream" date night?</u>

<u>If someone gave you $2500 to spend however you please, what would you do with it?</u>

<u>What is the best date or trip we have ever been on?</u>

<u>What is the best gift you ever received in life? What's the best gift you've ever received from me? Why?</u>

<u>When did you first know that you loved me?</u>

<u>What is the most important thing that you feel that you do in an average day?</u>

<u>Is our physical relationship what you hoped it would be? Why or why not?</u>

<u>What do you like best about being married to me?</u>

<u>Tell each other something special about each other that the average person may not see.</u>

FREE DATES

Walking is always a romantic date. Holding hands as you walk makes it that much better. Talk about what's going right in your life. Take a walk on a Riverwalk, marina, or near a lake. Find a beautiful setting in a park or any favorite spot.

Plan an old fashioned picnic. It doesn't matter if it's at a park or in your backyard, or in your living room. Pack your favorite foods. A picnic never loses its romance.

Have a game night. Pull out any board game or find a game on the internet for two. You can even make it interesting, by playing a strip version of the game in the privacy of your bedroom.

Explore your own city. Find local jewels. Go see the shops downtown or in your neighborhood.

Read a book together. Check out a book at the library or in your Kindle library. Take turns reading. Leave time to discuss the story.

Make a candlelight dinner with only the food that is available in the house. Make it interesting.

Write a vision statement for your family and your marriage. Starting out it won't be perfect. It takes time to tweak it and get it where you want it. After you have your statement add some things you want to see in your family. For example: family vacations once a year, family dinners once a week.

Give each other full body massages. Set the atmosphere. Light scented candles. Add chocolate. Play music in the background and enjoy.

Play one on one basketball in the driveway or backyard. Even if you have no skills, this is a fun date for a married couple.

- Be kids at heart. Go to a park and swing on the swings and go down the slide. Make a contest out of it.

- Play hide and seek in the dark. If the seeker finds the hider within a certain time limit, he/she must give up something. (a kiss, a hug, an article of clothing).

- Have a romantic candlelight bubble bath. Whether you have jetted tub or not, this date always pleases. Play music and enjoy.

- Have a cooking date. Cook a creative dish together. Make sure it's something different. You both have to eat it when it's done.

- Explore wineries/vineyards. Some have picnic areas, hiking trails, and fountains. Take your own lunch.

Phone Photography. Set a theme. Drive out to the perfect setting and take unique pictures with your phone and compare at the end of the date.

Spend the night by the fireplace talking about your dream vacation or dream home.

Play doctor.

Find a free lecture or event to attend at a local college.

Make homemade ice cream together.

Spend the day at the beach.

Play dodge ball in the basement or backyard. You could also play this in the living room with a beach ball.

🔥 If you are the outdoors-type, exploring the outdoors by hiking would make a great date.

🔥 Create your love story in pictures in a scrapbook. Be sure to play your favorite music in the background for inspiration.

🔥 Take a free class at Home Depot. Work on a project together.

🔥 Name that tune. Play love songs from the year you got married and each of you try to guess with just a few notes.

🔥 Power walking around a track early in the morning together is not only healthy living but healthy loving.

🔥 Set up a tent in your living room. Camp out. Roast marshmallows in the fireplace.

Watch the sunrise or sunset

Build a snowman together.

See an outdoor movie. Most are free. But bundle up, temps tend to be cooler in the evenings.

Find a spot and people watch. Make up stories about what you imagine their lives to be like.

Have a snowball fight.

Go to a poetry reading. Then write your own poems for each other.

Spy out the land. Test drive your dream vehicle or tour your dream house. Or just drive around the ritzy part of town.

Workout together. Grab a DVD or

Youtube video and get going.

✺ Complete a jigsaw puzzle together.

✺ Get dressed up in your wedding garb and recite new vows for each other.

✺ Prepare breakfast in bed for your spouse.

✺ Sit by a bonfire. Enjoy smores, hot cocoa, or roasted marshmallows.

✺ Water gun or water balloon fights in the backyard.

✺ A night of exploration. Get a flashlight and some oils and explore each other's bodies. Either start out nude or peel off the layers.

✺ Grab a blanket and gaze at the stars.

- If you are have ever considered bringing an animal into your family, browse your local pet store. This is not a time to purchase unless you both just fall in love with a pet and agree.

- Attend a fireworks display.

- Movie fest: Prepare your favorite snacks ahead of time. Alternate watching movies he picked and she picked.

- Go swimming together. If you can't swim, just play in the water.

- During the holidays, drive through neighborhoods looking at Christmas lights and displays.

DATES ON A DIME

(Low Budget)

Oscar & Crystal Jones

- Meet at a coffee shop for coffee/tea. Talk about your biggest dream. If money were no object, I would...

- Go thrifting. Set a budget and go treasure hunting at a resale shop or garage sale. Find something special for each other.

- Catch a morning matinee.

- Invite your spouse in to try your favorite hobby. Often spouses keep each other off limits in this arena. This will draw you closer to one another. (scrapbooking, collecting, chess, etc.).

- Fly a kite together.

- Go to a drive-in movie. Cuddle and enjoy the movie.

- Go to the Apple Orchard/Cider Mill. Don't forget to take the hayride.

- Take a mini road trip no further than 1.5 hours away in either direction.

- Purchase some canvas and paints. Make up your own theme and paint. You don't have to be an artist to enjoy this one. For a nice touch, add music in the background.

- Find a botanical garden. Walk through holding hands.

- Spend the night doing karaoke. Serenade each other.

- Hit golf balls at the driving range. Helping her with her swing is a great opportunity to get up close and personal.

- Take a bike ride together. Ride separate bikes or one bike built for two.

- Go out for frozen yogurt or ice cream.

- Go bowling.

- Visit a local museum or art gallery.

- Make a ceramic item together in a pottery class.

- Enjoy a day at the zoo.

- Meet out at your favorite dessert spot. Feed each other.

- Go to an auto/boat/or house show.

- Go snowmobiling, sledding

- Locate a Christian Comedy show to enjoy.

- Try miniature golf.

Take a tram, bus ride, train, or trolley around the city.

Visit an arcade. Compete in pinball, Pac Man, and other vintage games.

Tour a castle or other famous site.

Become recording artists. Sing a song together or rap. The cd will be a keepsake for years to come.

Write the story of how you met. Get it printed and bound.

Go-cart racing is loads of fun. Bring out the child in yourself and your spouse.

Take a tour of local attractions and famous sites.

Go to a sports bar and watch the game together.

- Shoot pool with your spouse.

- Participate in a mud run.

- Try a one on one sport together like tennis, volleyball, badminton, etc.

- Visit a senior in your life and take a special homemade gift. Ask him/her to impart wisdom in your marriage.

Oscar & Crystal Jones

OTHER FUN DATES

Oscar & Crystal Jones

- Recreate your first date.

- Go skiing. Better yet, take lessons then go skiing.

- Learn to dance. Take dancing lessons. Enjoy the journey but once the classes are completed, then go out to show off your new skills.

- Attend sporting events. Take a blanket, wear your team's jersey and have some fun.

- Take a cooking class.

- Attend a carnival or state fair.

- Dress up and go to a fancy restaurant

- Go boating, paddle boating, or canoeing. Lots of boat tours are offered through daily discount sites like Groupon and LivingSocial; look for a sunset one for ultimate romantic ambiance.

- Enjoy a drive-thru safari.

- Get tickets to the circus. No children needed to enjoy.

- Go to an indoor or outdoor amusement park.

- Take a dj class. Find coupons on Groupon or LivingSocial.

- Schedule a couples massage.

- See a play or musical.

- Revisit your honeymoon spot.

- Take a dinner cruise.

- Go ice skating, rollerblading, or rollerskating. Even if you don't know how, you can still have fun.

- Play laser tag.

- Go out for a fast paced date of Whirlyball.

- Venture to DisneyWorld/Disneyland without the children. Enjoy yourselves.

- Go to a ballet, opera, or symphony. Even if you are not a connoisseur, do it just for fun.

- Head to the shooting range for a quick lesson and target practice.

- Go golfing. If one of you is not interested, he/she can drive the golf cart.

- Take a spinning class together.

- Go horseback riding for a fun date.

- Try archery.

- Dinner theatre or mystery theatre is a cut from the norm.

- Take a motorcycle ride. Make sure have your helmets and follow safety tips.

- Enjoy a carriage ride through the city.

- Enroll in a sculpting class.

- Create a music video together.

- Some of the more adventurous couples would enjoy rock climbing. Make sure you both are up for it. This is not an activity in which you "surprise" your spouse.

- Visit an aquarium.

- Ziplining could also be fun for couples who aren't afraid of heights.

- Take a dinner train ride if they are available in your area.

- Enjoy a jazz concert together. Or a different genre of music that you two have in common.

- Snorkeling is a great water sport for dating. You don't have to know how to swim to snorkel.

- Take a helicopter ride.

- Purchase cheap airline tickets to a nearby destination. Fly in for dinner and enjoy the city.

Take a hot air balloon ride.

ROMANTIC GETAWAYS

Oscar & Crystal Jones

It's important that couples take the time to steal away to keep the embers burning in their relationship. Any get away can be romantic. It can be as simple as getting away at a bed and breakfast for one night in a small town. Or as elaborate as the two of you can imagine.

Couples should financially prepare to get away at least twice a year. We recommend 'weekend' getaways to start out. However, it is good to aim at getting away together for longer periods of time as your budget allows. We have composed a list of romantic spots. This list is not exhaustive. There are plenty of romantic getaways in this country and abroad. These are just a few of the places we've found romance in.

Atlanta {Lake Lanier} (Georgia)

Atlantic City Boardwalk (New Jersey)

Aruba

Nassau, Bahamas

Boca Raton (Florida)

Curacao

Carmel By The Sea (California)

Cayman Islands

Chattanooga (Tennessee)

Chicago Downtown (Illinois)

Cozumel, Mexico

Cruising anywhere, any ship

Detroit Downtown & Riverwalk (Michigan)

Fort Lauderdale (Florida)

Frankenmuth (Michigan)

Gatlinburg (Tennessee)

Hawaiian islands (any)

Hilton Head (South Carolina)

Lake Tahoe (Nevada)

Lovers Point (California)

Mackinaw Island (Michigan)

Montego Bay (Jamaica)

Monterey Wharf (California)

Myrtle Beach (North Carolina)

Napa Valley (California)

New Orleans (Louisiana)

New York City (New York)

Niagara Falls (Canada or NY)

Oakland Downtown (California)

Ocho Rios, Jamaica

Pocono Mountains (Pennsylvania)

San Antonio River Walk(Texas)

San Diego (California)

San Francisco Wharf (California)

San Juan, Puerto Rico

Santa Cruz Beach (California)

Savannah (Georgia)

St. Thomas (U.S. Virgin Islands)

St. Kitts

Toronto, Canada

Traverse City (Michigan)

U.S. Virgin Islands

Venice Beach (California)

Wisconsin Dells (Wisconsin)

ABOUT THE AUTHORS

Oscar & Crystal Jones have been celebrating their covenant love for nearly 33 years. Their passion for one another has yielded a great harvest. They have 7 children. Two of which are bonus children who married into their family: Jake & Keila, Kyria, Charity & Erik, LaTina, and Christopher. They also delight in their 6 precious grandchildren with a set of twins joining the brood in January.

Oscar & Crystal are both teachers by trade. They have taught in both the private and public sectors. Oscar has taught for both Detroit Public Schools and the Oakland Unified School District. He left teaching after 27 years to pursue fulltime ministry. Crystal is a licensed and practicing realtor for Professional Realty.

Pastors Oscar & Crystal have an apostolic and prophetic mandate. They oversee **Greater Works Family Ministries** in Detroit, MI**, Marriage For A Lifetime Ministries**. They are founders of **Agape International Association of Churches and Parachurches** and overseers to **The Love Culture Christian Center in Atlanta, GA**

They are serious about encouraging and supporting marriages. They host a monthly teleconference call to strengthen marriages. They have also been featured guests on several radio and television broadcasts.

The couple has authored and co-authored several books. These long-time honeymooners continue to have a passion for marriage ministry. They have a unique team ministry where they speak together as one voice. They are in demand as conference speakers.

The couple currently resides in Atlanta, GA area where they enjoy spending time with each other.

Contact Information:

Marriage For A Lifetime Ministries
Oscar & Crystal Jones
P.O. Box 19774
Detroit, MI 48219
Email: jones@marriage4alifetime.org
Website: www.marriage4alifetime.org
Phone: 920.474.MFAL (6325)

OTHER BOOKS BY THE AUTHORS

A Woman's Place: Leading Ladies Speak Compiled by Crystal Jones & Joceline Bronson

Extreme Money Makeover by Oscar & Crystal Jones

Fast Food for the Married Soul by Oscar & Crystal Jones

Heart of the Roar by Oscar Jones

I Want A Husband, Too by Crystal Jones

LeaderShift 3.0 by Oscar & Crystal Jones

Naked Sex (For Married Couples Only) by Oscar & Crystal Jones

No Longer A Dream: Step by Step Guide to Writing Your First Book
-by Crystal Jones

Not Without My Daughters: The Beginner's Guide to Mentoring and Being Mentored by Crystal Jones

Restore The Roar by Oscar Jones

Ring Talks by Oscar & Crystal Jones

The Newlywed Handbook by Oscar & Crystal Jones

No Longer A Dream: Step by Step Guide to Writing Your First Book by Crystal Jones

The S Word: What Submission Is Not by Crystal Jones

When The Vow Breaks by Oscar & Crystal Jones